Christmas with Kevin Costley

OK 1 - Late Elementary/Early Intermediate

Compiled and Arranged by Kevin Costley

Kevin Costley

Dr. Kevin Costley holds several graduate degrees in the areas of curriculum, instruction, and piano pedagogy/literature, including a Ph.D. from Kansas State University. At the age of 27, he was distinguished as one of K-State's youngest doctors. For nearly two decades, he was owner/director of the Keyboard Academy, specializing in private and small group teaching.

Since 1995, Dr. Costley has been a standing faculty member at Inspiration Point Fine Arts Colony Piano and String Camp, where he specializes in large ensemble classes and teaching composition. His published compositions have been continually listed in the National Federation of Music Clubs bulletins, the Royal Conservatory list, and other performance repertoire lists. He was awarded the Certificate of Merit in California for his Composer in Focus collections published by The FJH Music Company, Inc. In 2008, Dr. Costley was awarded the prestigious Arkansas Traveler's Award by the governor and commissioner of the state of Arkansas in recognition of his distinguished accomplishments in the field of piano composition. Frequently Dr. Costley adjudicates piano festivals, auditions, and composition contests and has been a speaker/clinician at state, regional, national and international conferences.

In 2011, Dr. Costley celebrated his silver anniversary with his wife, Dana. He is the father of two musical children, Benjamin (a percussionist) and Victoria (a pianist). After retiring from university teaching in 2015, he now resides back in his home state of Missouri. He and his wife became proud, first-time grandparents in 2016.

For more information including videos and published music, visit www.kevincostley.com.

Production: Frank J. Hackinson
Production Coordinators: Peggy Gallagher and Philip Groeber
Editor: Edwin McLean
Cover Layout: Andi Whitmer
Engraving: Tempo Music Press, Inc.
Printer: Tempo Music Press, Inc.

THE FJH MUSIC COMPANY INC.
Frank J. Hackinson

ISBN-13: 978-1-61928-196-7

MW00680352

2

A Note to Students

Christmas is a very popular holiday for all who celebrate this joyous day. In fact, it is so well-loved, the Hallmark television channel broadcasts Christmas movies every July and also during the entire months of November and December. Christmas is a much anticipated holiday; merchandizers begin putting up decorations to sell in early August.

As always, my thoughts go back to my joyous childhood Christmases. When I was ten years old, my twin brother and I arose early Christmas morning. We ran down the stairs to see what was under the tree. We both screamed with shock and delight to see two shiny red Western Flyer bikes. I've since restored my old, weathered bike; it now looks like new!

Because of the joy of this holiday, I truly enjoy arranging Christmas piano music. Christmas music never gets old to me. As you play through all three collections of *Christmas with Kevin Costley,* I hope these familiar arrangements remind you of your fondest memories of Christmas. Keep making more memories and . . .

Merry Christmas!

Kevin Costley

CONTENTS

4

I Saw Three Ships

Traditional

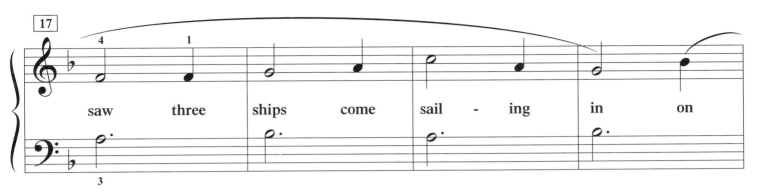

saw three ships come sail - ing in on

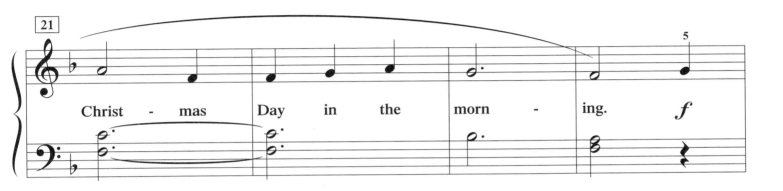

Christ - mas Day in the morn - ing. *f*

dim. e rit.

a tempo

p

5

6

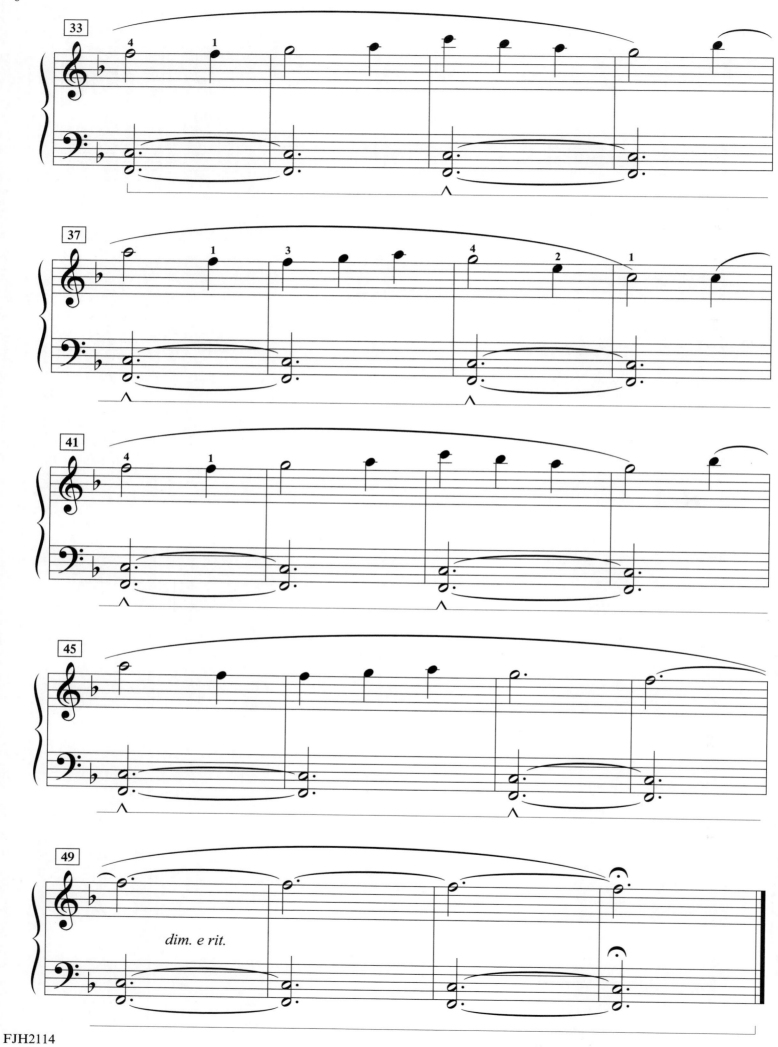

dim. e rit.

Jolly Old Saint Nicholas

Traditional

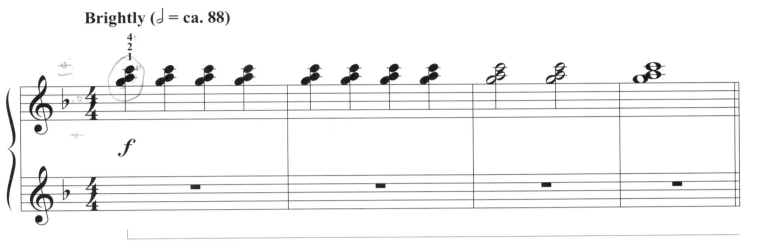

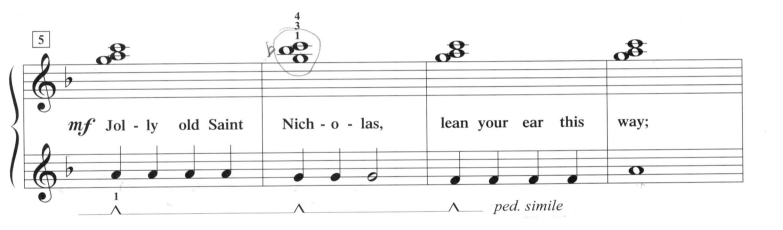

Jol - ly   old Saint   Nich - o - las,   lean your ear this   way;

Don't you tell   a   sin - gle soul   what I'm going to   say.

FJH2114

8

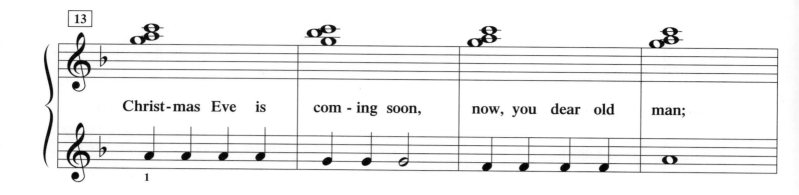

Christ-mas Eve is com - ing soon, now, you dear old man;

Whis - per what you'll bring to me, tell me if you can.

mp John - ny wants a pair of skates; Su - sy wants a sled.

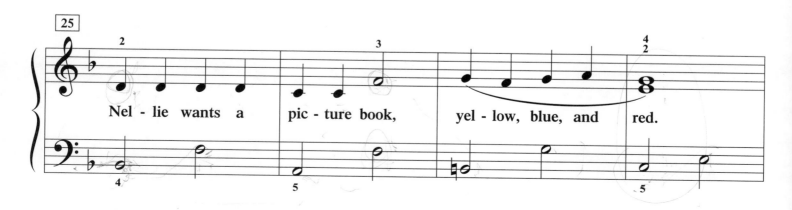

Nel - lie wants a pic - ture book, yel - low, blue, and red.

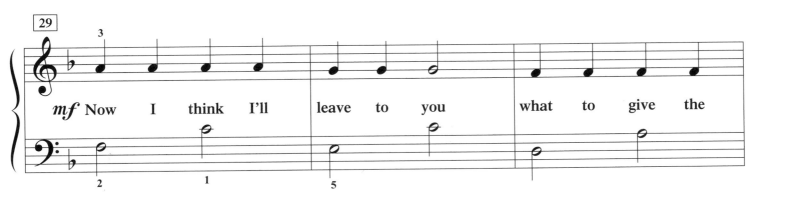

29 *mf* Now I think I'll leave to you what to give the

32 rest; Choose for me, dear San - ta Claus,

35 you will know the best. *f*

38 *p*

Jingle Bells

James Pierpont

Happily (♩ = ca. 80)

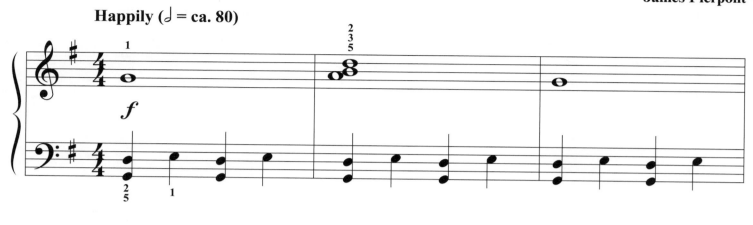

Dash - ing through the snow in a

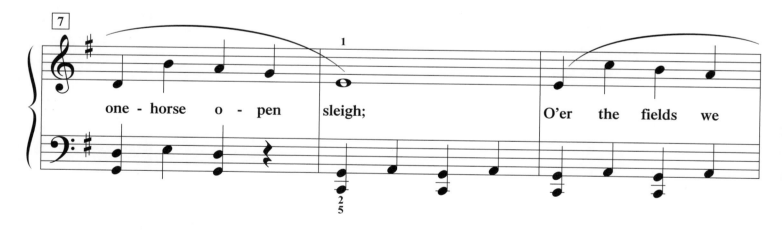

one - horse o - pen sleigh; O'er the fields we

go, laugh - ing all the way.

Bells on bob - tail nag, mak - ing spir - its

bright; What fun it is to ride and

cresc.

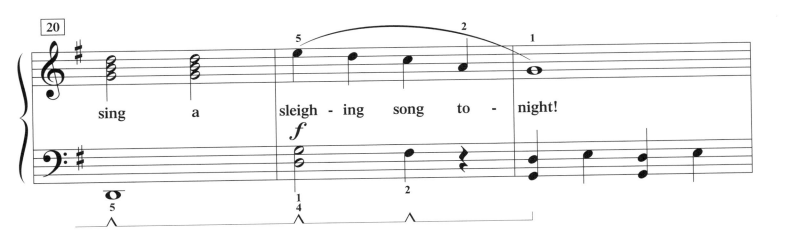

sing a sleigh - ing song to - night!

f

12

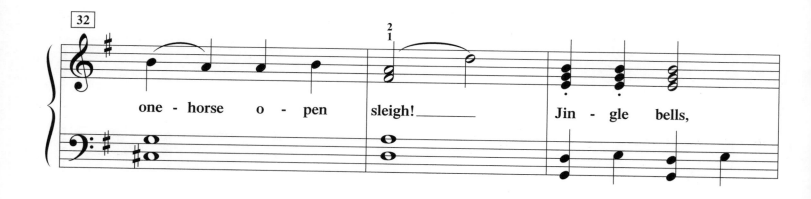

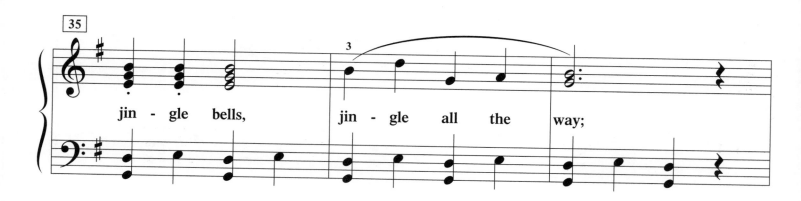

FJH2114

Oh, what fun it is to ride in a one - horse o - pen

sleigh!

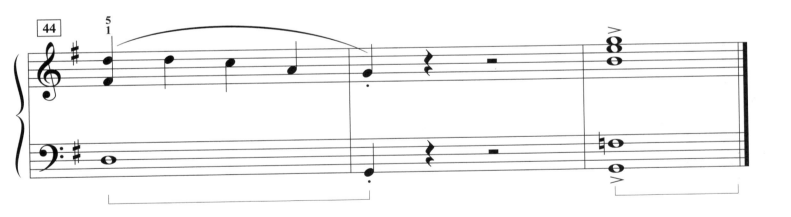

God Rest Ye Merry, Gentlemen

Traditional English Carol

God rest ye mer - ry, gen - tle - men, let noth - ing you dis - may; Re - mem - ber Christ our Sav - iour was born on Christ - mas Day. To

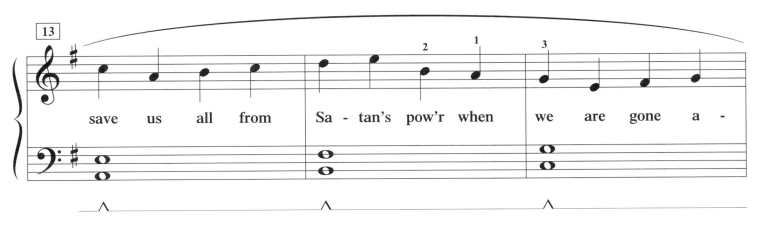

save us all from Sa - tan's pow'r when we are gone a -

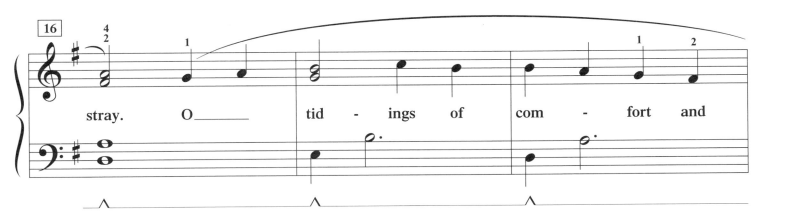

stray. O_____ tid - ings of com - fort and

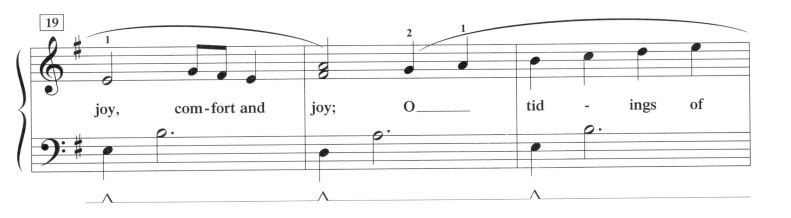

joy, com-fort and joy; O_____ tid - ings of

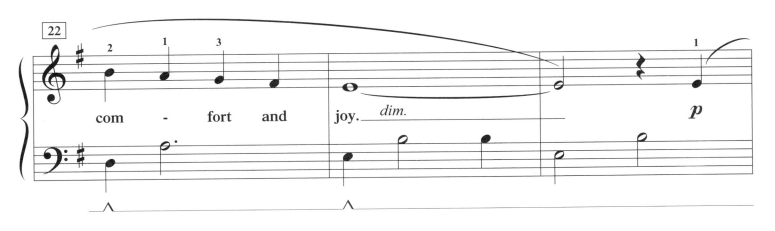

com - fort and joy. *dim.* _____ *p*

O Christmas Tree
(O Tannenbaum)

German Folk Song

Moderato con moto (♩ = 96)

O Christ-mas tree, O Christ-mas tree, your

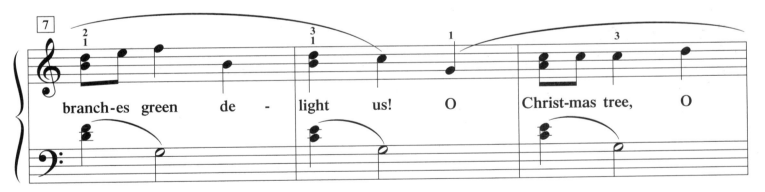

branch-es green de - light us! O Christ-mas tree, O

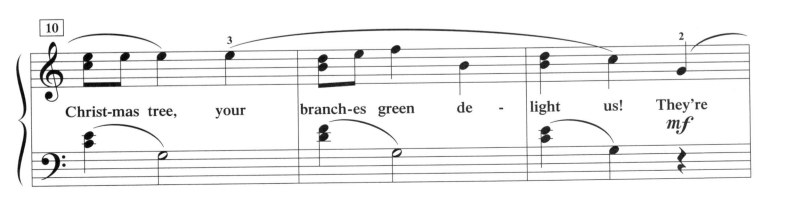

Christ-mas tree, your branch-es green de - light us! They're

FJH2114

green when sum - mer days are bright: They're green when win - ter

snow is white. O Christ-mas tree, O Christ-mas tree, your

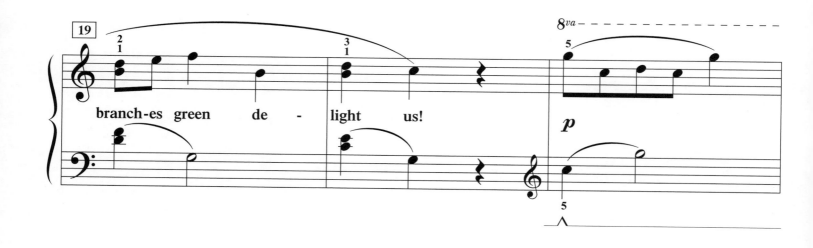

branch-es green de - light us!

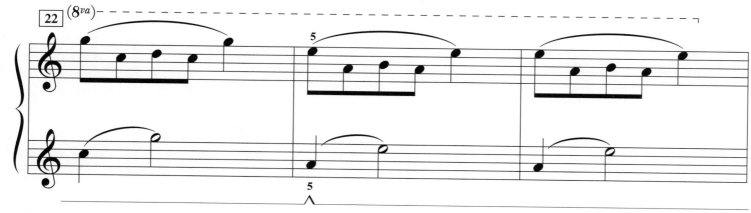

Silent Night
(Stille Nacht)

Lyrics by Joseph Mohr
Music by Franz Gruber

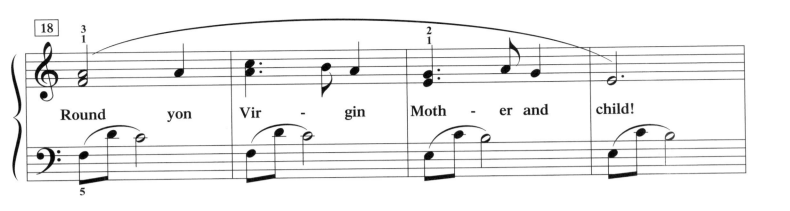

Round   yon   Vir - gin   Moth - er and   child!

Ho - ly   In - fant so   ten - der and   mild,

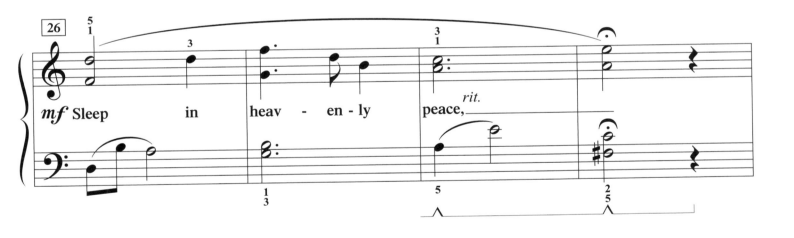

mf Sleep   in   heav - en - ly   peace,____ *rit.*

a tempo

Sleep____   in   heav - en - ly   peace.

ped. simile

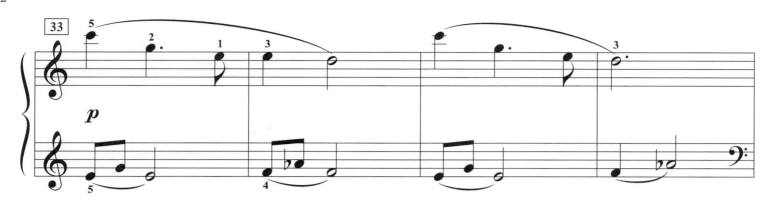

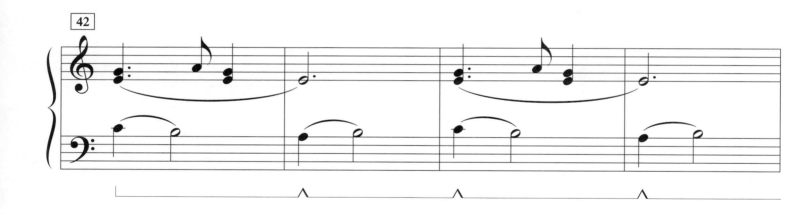

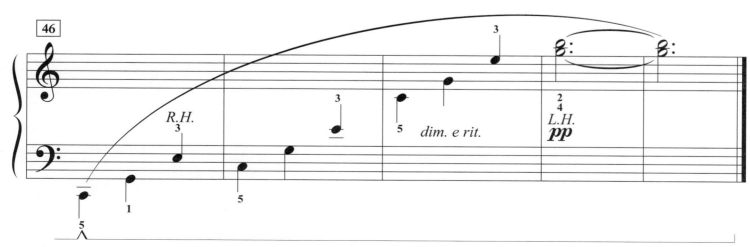

Up On the Housetop

Benjamin R. Hanby

Moving along quickly (𝅗𝅥 = ca. 76)

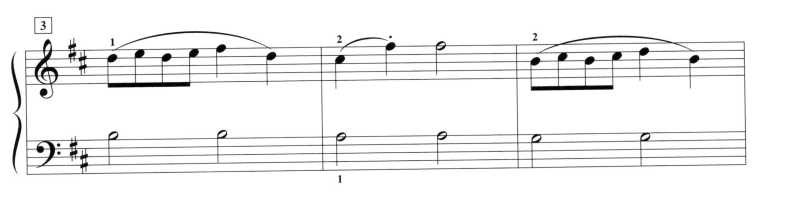

24

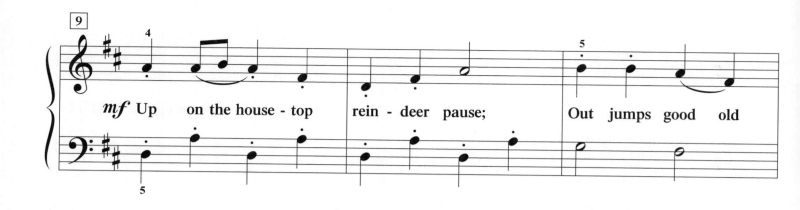

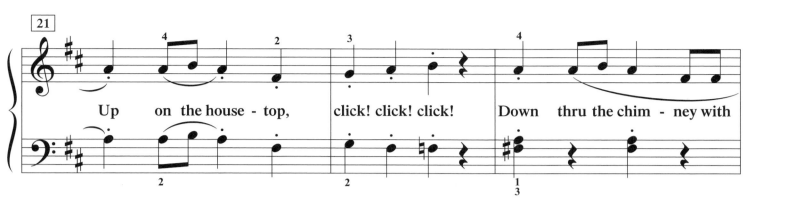

Up   on the house - top,   click! click! click!   Down   thru the chim - ney with

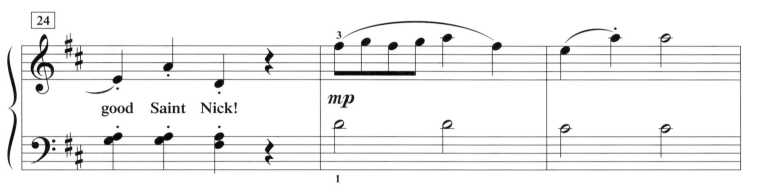

good   Saint Nick!

mp

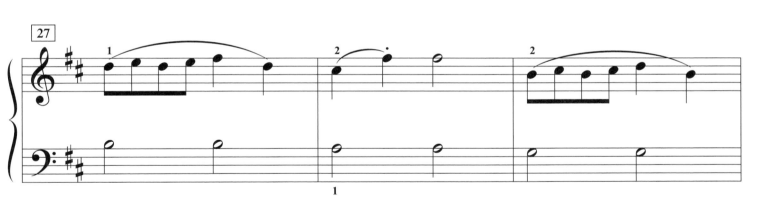

f

FJH2114

We Wish You a Merry Christmas

Traditional English Carol

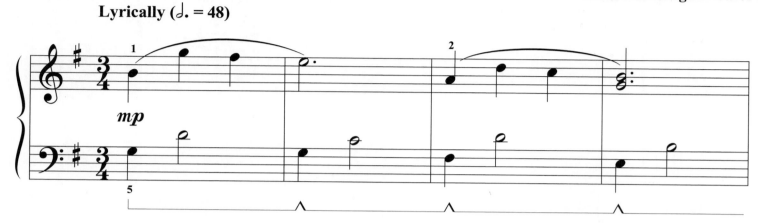

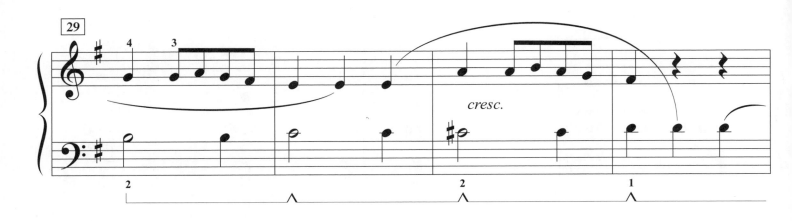

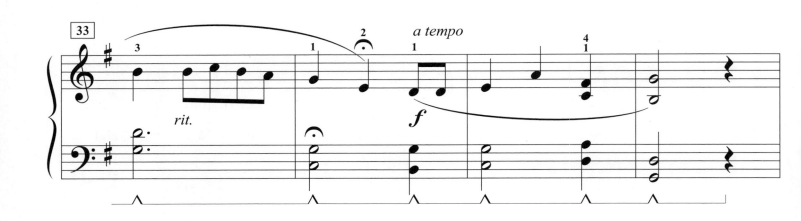

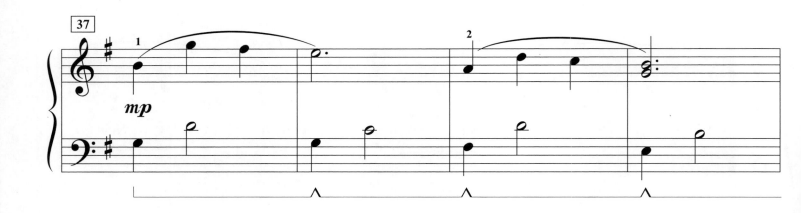

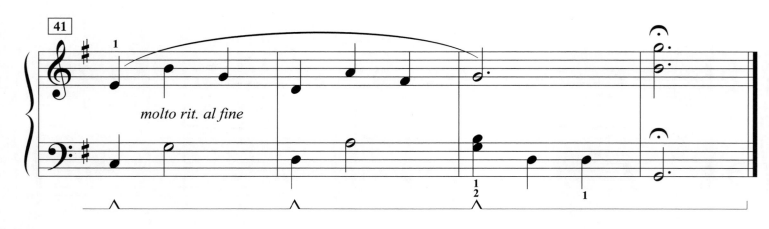